D0851963

MARY LOU RETTON

SISKIYOU COUNTY SCHOOLS LIBRARY

MARY LOU RETTON

POWER GYMNAST

Rosemary G. Washington

Lerner Publications Company ■ Minneapolis

LIBRARY OF CONGRESS CATALOGING IN PUBLICATION DATA

Washington, Rosemary G.
    Mary Lou Retton: power gymnast.

    (The Achievers)
    Summary: Follows the training and career of Mary Lou Retton, the
first American woman gymnast to win a gold medal in the Olympics.

    1. Retton, Mary Lou, 1968-   —Juvenile literature. 2. Gymnasts—
United States—Biography—Juvenile literature. 3. Olympic Games (23rd:
1984: Los Angeles, Calif.)—Juvenile literature. [1. Retton, Mary Lou,
1968-   . 2. Gymnasts. 3. Olympic Games (23rd: 1984: Los Angeles,
Calif.)] I. Title. II. Series.

GV460.2.R47W37   1985   796.4′1′0924 [B] [92]   84-29003
ISBN 0-8225-0497-9 (lib. bdg.)

Copyright © 1985 by Lerner Publications Company

All rights reserved. International copyright secured. No part of this book
may be reproduced in any form whatsoever without permission in writing from the
publisher except for the inclusion of brief quotations in an acknowledged review.

Manufactured in the United States of America

International Standard Book Number: 0-8225-0497-9
Library of Congress Catalog Card Number: 84-29003

2   3   4   5   6   7   8   9   10   94   93   92   91   90   89   88   87   86   85

MARY LOU RETTON: POWER GYMNAST

The setting was Pauley Pavilion at the University of Southern California in Los Angeles. The time was the 1984 Olympic Games. Before a sellout crowd of more than 9,000 cheering fans, 16-year-old Mary Lou Retton bounded into the record books as the first United States' woman gymnast ever to win a gold medal in Olympic competition!

In achieving her gold medal, Retton had broken the mold of the other great woman gymnasts who had come before her. At 4 feet, 10 inches and 95 pounds, Mary Lou's muscular frame did not resemble the lithe figure of the classical gymnast. Instead she was strong, powerful, and athletic. She set a new standard for daring and athletic routines, a standard that replaced the more graceful, ballet style of former gymnasts.

5

Retton admitted she simply was not suited to the older, lyrical style. "I couldn't go out doing a floor routine ballet-style or something," she said. "I have to have strong and powerful music and do lots of leaps and jumps." Bela Karolyi, Mary Lou's coach, said, "She became the number-one representative of a new trend in gymnastics, a trend of high difficulty and very athletic stunts."

Not many athletes have the overpowering talent to become trend setters, but Mary Lou pulled it off. Her stunning moves, explosive power, and daring stunts were breathtaking. During the Olympics, one sports commentator described her as "a jalapeno pepper with the smile of an angel." She won admirers all over the world with her unbelievable energy and gutsy, competitive spirit.

Mary Lou had learned to be a determined competitor when she was growing up in Fairmont, West Virginia. She was the youngest of five children in an athletic family. Her two oldest brothers, Ronnie and Donnie, played baseball in college. Her youngest brother, Jerry, still in high school, lettered in three sports. And her sister, Shari, was an All-American gymnast at college.

Mary Lou had started gymnastics training when she was only 7 years old. Never still, Retton was always getting into things, climbing on furniture, jumping from fences, or running around the house. Her parents sent her to ballet and acrobatics classes to direct some of her boundless energy.

Retton enjoyed gymnastics from the start and began competing internationally when she was 14. In one of her first meets, the 1982 Sanlam Cup Invitational in South Africa, Mary Lou defeated gymnasts from South Africa, West Germany, Israel, Denmark, and Austria and placed first in every event! But because she had not yet faced the world's top-ranked gymnasts, her actual potential was not generally recognized.

In 1982, the best woman gymnast in the world was Natalia Yurchenko of the Soviet Union. Natalia, a graceful, slender gymnast, performed with beautiful artistry and expression. She also had the strength to execute the most difficult routines. One of the innovative vaulting maneuvers that showed off her originality and exceptional talent was a round-off back handspring onto the horse. That year, Yurchenko didn't lose a single competition.

The top-ranked United States' gymnast and the 1983 national champion was Dianne Durham, a black athlete from Gary, Indiana. Dianne's speciality was the floor exercise. Like Retton, she was a powerful, muscular gymnast who was capable of performing difficult tumbling moves.

Dianne Durham is congratulated by her young fans after winning the 1983 U.S.A. Gymnastics Championships.

But Durham and Retton had more in common than just their physical stature. Both trained under the same coach, Bela Karolyi. Karolyi's credentials were impressive. He had discovered Nadia Comaneci, coaching her to her Olympic triumph in 1976. And he had built the strong Rumanian team that ended the U.S.S.R. domination of the sport. In 1981, Karolyi and his wife, Marta, defected from Rumania and established a gymnastics training center in Houston, Texas.

Coach Bela Karolyi with Nadia Comaneci at the 1976 Olympics

Karolyi's arrival in the United States had coincided with Mary Lou's search for a new coach. By 1982, Retton had outgrown the competitive environment in West Virginia. From coach Gary Rafalowski, she had acquired a solid foundation in gymnastics and had advanced to the elite level, the division from which the national gymnastics team is selected. But Mary Lou was the only elite gymnast in West Virginia, and she felt that she needed to train with others at that level in order to keep improving.

In early 1983, Retton left West Virginia for Houston to train under Karolyi. He taught her how to use her tremendous power, and together they perfected her difficult routines. Karolyi's methods were intense, demanding, and repetitious. Mary Lou trained seven days a week with two long sessions each day.

The rigorous training demanded a lot of sacrifices. Mary Lou had to leave her family and home, and she dropped out of public school and switched to correspondence courses after her freshman year. As a result, she missed the social life of high school. But Retton felt the sacrifices were worthwhile. She was determined to become a great gymnast and was driven by the desire for an Olympic medal. She worked hard and improved dramatically under Karolyi's coaching, and her routines reflected her growing self-confidence and the belief that her efforts would someday be

11

SISKIYOU COUNTY SCHOOLS LIBRARY

recognized. Her workouts with other elite gymnasts challenged her to try even harder, and she and Dianne Durham soon developed a friendly rivalry. "We are good friends," said Retton, "But there is a feeling that if she can do it, I can do it. If she does well, then *I* have to do well, too."

Ironically, Mary Lou's big break in gymnastics came when she substituted for Dianne at the 1983 McDonald's American Cup in New York City's Madison Square Garden. Retton was still not well known in the international circuit and had not been invited. Durham, who was scheduled to represent the United States, unexpectedly suffered a last-minute injury, and Retton was selected to replace her.

Retton utterly dominated the meet. She won the all-around title and took gold medals in the floor exercise, the vault, and the uneven bars. Moreover, she resoundingly defeated Natalia Yurchenko, the reigning world champion. Her unexpected victories shot Mary Lou into the international limelight. Said Karolyi, "It was the greatest shock of 1983—a complete unknown in the American Cup beating everyone else in the world!"

Some skeptics, however, thought Retton's victory was a fluke. They believed Yurchenko had been caught off guard. Would the outcome have been the same if the Soviet gymnast had been prepared for

Mary Lou's powerful style of competition? That controversy generated a great deal of interest in the next scheduled Retton-Yurchenko confrontation, the 1983 World Championships in Budapest, Hungary. Unfortunately, Mary Lou, suffering from a stress fractured left wrist, had to miss the competition, and Dianne Durham was also injured.

Without its two best gymnasts, the United States struggled to a seventh-place team finish. The U.S.S.R. and Rumania dominated the championships and finished first and second, respectively. Natalia Yurchenko won the all-around event with perfect scores of 10 on the vault, the beam, and in the floor exercise. She also retained her title of "world's best gymnast."

In the months between the World Championships and the Olympics, a recovered Mary Lou valiantly fought to re-establish her credentials as a leading international competitor. At the Chunichi Cup Invitational in Japan, she came away with the all-around title, the first U.S. woman to win in the 13-year history of the competition. In winning, Retton defeated several world-class gymnasts, including Maxi Gnauck of the German Democratic Republic, Elena Shoushounova of the Soviet Union, and teammate Dianne Durham, who finished third all-around. Mary Lou also won the gold medal on the vault by defeating Boriana Stoyanova of Bulgaria, the reigning world titlist.

At the 1983 World Championships, Natalia Yurchenko scored a perfect 10 on the balance beam.

In 1984, a high-flying Mary Lou Retton won the all-around event at the McDonald's American Cup for the second year in a row.

Then in March 1984, Retton repeated her McDonald's American Cup victory by winning the all-around title for the second consecutive year. She received perfect 10s in both the floor exercise and on the uneven bars.

During the events leading up to the Olympics, the meeting between Retton and Natalia Yurchenko never took place. Yurchenko was absent from both the Chunichi Cup and the McDonald's American Cup. Los Angeles, site of the 1984 Olympic Games, was to be the arena for their confrontation.

15

Unfortunately, the anticipated battle between the two gymnasts was postponed one more time when the U.S.S.R. announced that its athletes were boycotting the Games. The Soviet gymnastic team included world champion Natalia Yurchenko; Olga Mostepanova, silver medalist in the 1983 World Championships; the 1983 European champion, Olga Bicherova; and other talented performers. Because of the boycott, Mary Lou Retton would be deprived of the challenge of facing some of her strongest opponents.

A shadow of speculation will always cloud the results of the 1984 Olympic Games because of the absence of top gymnasts like Natalia Yurchenko. But critics still had to agree that the United States had become a major contender in international gymnastics.

Before the 1984 Games, there had been few world-class gymnasts in the United States. The first and only American woman to win an individual gold medal in world-caliber competition had been Marcia Fredericks, who scored a perfect 10 on the uneven bars at the 1978 World Championships in Yugoslavia. Her teammate at the competition, Kathy Johnson, won the bronze medal in the floor exercise. Their efforts helped the United States to a fifth-place team finish.

Although she never won a gold medal in the World Championships or in the Olympic Games, Cathy Rigby was perhaps the best-known U.S. gymnast to precede

Mary Lou. Cathy was only 15 years old in 1968 when she made the U.S.A. team for the first time. Because she was the youngest member of the team, some thought of the 4-foot, 11-inch blonde sprite as little more than a team mascot. But Rigby made a strong contribution to the team and finished 16th in the all-around final. More important, she gained valuable experience in international competition.

Two years later, that experience paid off. At the 1970 World Championships, Cathy was awarded a silver medal on the beam, the first individual medal ever won by an American gymnast in international competition. Overnight, she became a celebrity, appearing on the cover of *Life* magazine and on numerous television shows. More than a decade later, Rigby still made television commercials and served as a commentator during the Olympics.

Cathy Rigby's achievement gave the U.S.A. good reason to hope for their first individual medal in Olympic gymnastics. But although she was a seasoned performer by the time of the 1972 Games, Rigby did not walk away with any medals in Munich. Instead, Olga Korbut and Ludmila Tourischeva of the U.S.S.R. stole the show. Cathy finished 10th in the all-around competition but helped the U.S.A. team place 4th, their best showing since 1948, when the U.S. women had finished 3rd.

Specializing in the balance beam *(above)* and on the uneven bars, Cathy Rigby was the U.S.A.'s best woman gymnast at the 1976 Olympics.

An Olympic medal eluded the U.S.A. team again in 1976 when Nadia Comaneci and the powerful Rumanian team dominated the Montreal Games. And hopes were dashed once more four years later when

18

President Jimmy Carter announced the U.S.A. boycott of the 1980 Moscow Olympics. When 1984 rolled around, Mary Lou Retton and her teammates were the United States' best hope for its first Olympic medal.

At the 1976 Olympics, Nadia Comaneci earned the first perfect score ever awarded in Olympic history.

The balance beam, only four inches wide, provides a very narrow "floor" for Retton's routine.

The gymnastics competition at the 1984 Olympics was a colorful event that resembled a four-ring circus. Women athletes competed in four areas: the balance beam, the uneven parallel bars, the vault, and the floor exercise.

The beam is approximately 4 inches wide and 16 feet long, and it stands 4 feet off the ground. On the beam, gymnasts perform tumbling and dance moves during routines that are from 75 to 90 seconds long.

The beam is sometimes called a "reduced floor" because gymnasts perform many of the same tumbling and dance moves on both apparatus. During the floor exercise, however, athletes can perform with much more abandon because they are not limited to a 4-inch wide area. The floor routine is done on a mat that is about 40 feet square.

Other skills are required for routines on the uneven parallel bars. As they move quickly and gracefully from bar to bar, gymnasts perform whirling rotations, daring release moves, and stunning poses.

On the vault, the higher score of two attempts counts. Competitors race down a runway and take off from a springboard. Then they push off the vaulting horse into the air and perform complicated twists, somersaults, and other maneuvers before landing.

A gymnast's performance is rated by a panel of judges who award a score of 10 points for a perfect routine. The judges look for accuracy and style and fullness of movement. Errors like falling or taking an extra step on a landing will result in deductions of 1/10 of a point. But gymnasts can also earn bonus points for risk, difficulty, or originality in their routines.

The Olympic gymnastics competition has both team and individual events, so each gymnast performs four times on each apparatus. The first event is the compulsory segment. During the compulsory exercises, every gymnast performs the same routine. The scores earned for these required moves and stunts count for 50 percent of the team score and also count toward the individual all-around scores.

The second round of competition, the optional exercises, gives gymnasts the opportunity to perform moves of their own choice. Most optional routines include maneuvers that are flamboyant, daring, and graceful. The scores from the optional exercises make up the remaining 50 percent of the team score as well as part of each individual's all-around score.

The third phase of competition, the all-around final, determines the best gymnasts at the Olympics. Each competitor's combined compulsory and optional scores are halved and count as 50 percent of her final all-around score. The points earned during the third round on the apparatus count for the remaining 50 percent.

Mary Lou's powerful style and fearless leaps made the vault her best event.

The fourth and last part of the gymnastics competition is the individual event finals with gold, silver, and bronze medals awarded for performance on each apparatus. Truly talented gymnasts like Mary Lou Retton excel on all four pieces of apparatus, as did Ludmila Tourischeva, Olga Korbut, and Nadia Comaneci who preceded her.

Soviet gymnast Ludmila Tourischeva was the winner of the all-around competition at the 1972 Olympics.

Ludmila Tourischeva represented the classic Soviet gymnast who performed with beautiful ballet poses, fluid movement, and artistic expression. Tourischeva rose to international prominence when she won the 1970 World Championships. Two years later at the 1972 Munich Olympics, she won the all-around title. Tourischeva continued to dominate women's gymnastics until the 1975 European Championships, when she was dethroned by Rumania's Nadia Comaneci.

Ludmila participated in her last Olympics in Montreal in 1976, where she won the bronze medal in the all-around competition and two silver medals in the individual events finals. Although she performed well on all of the apparatus, Tourischeva particularly excelled in the floor exercise.

While she was recognized as the superior gymnast on the Soviet team, Tourisheva was often overshadowed by her teammate, Olga Korbut. Seventeen-year-old Olga had stormed into the limelight at the 1972 Munich Olympics, where she won gold medals on the beam and floor exercise. Korbut revolutionized gymnastics with her originality, and she will always be remembered for her daring back flip on the high bar and her backward somersault on the beam. The latter move was nearly banned by gymnastics officials because they considered it so dangerous.

Olga Korbut, the gold medal winner in Munich, was known for
her daring moves on the balance beam.

26

Today Korbut is still recognized as the one who popularized the sport of gymnastics, captivating audiences all over the world with her appealing gestures, wide-open smile, and pixie-like charm.

Nadia Comaneci of Rumania ended the Soviet domination of women's gymnastics. At 14, Comaneci became the youngest Olympic champion at the 1976 Montreal Games, where she performed so flawlessly that she was awarded the first perfect 10 in Olympic history! In fact, Nadia scored an unprecedented total of seven 10s during the Games and came away with the gold for the all-around competition, the uneven bars, and the beam, and a bronze medal in the floor exercise. Comaneci participated in her second Olympics in 1980. Although she placed second in the all-around competition, she won gold medals on the beam and in the floor exercise.

In 1984, the United States had selected one of its strongest Olympic gymnastics teams ever. For the first time, both the men's and the women's teams showed remarkable depth and experience. Several had also been members of the ill-fated 1980 team that was forced to miss the Games because of the U.S.A. boycott. On the men's team, Bart Conner was a three-time Olympic team member. And the women's team included three veteran performers from 1980: Julianne McNamara, Kathy Johnson, and Tracee Talavera.

Only six gymnasts and one alternate are allowed to represent each nation at the Olympics. The United States' team was selected in a two-stage process. The top finishers in the 1984 U.S.A. Championships advanced to the Olympic trials. Then their scores from the Championships and the trials were combined, and each woman's final score was determined by adding 40 percent of her Championship score to 60 percent of her trials score. The top eight gymnasts were sent to the Olympic training camp, but only the top four finishers were guaranteed spots on the Olympic team. The remaining two team members would be selected in mid-July after training camp from among the bottom four finishers, with the Olympic team coaches and United States Gymnastics Federation officials making the final cut.

Mary Lou won the number-one spot on the team. Soaring almost effortlessly through the trials, she earned the best optional scores and the second-best compulsory scores. (At both the U.S.A. Championships and the Olympic trials, the scores were based 60 percent on compulsory exercises and 40 percent on optional exercises.)

The trials did not prove so easy for some of the other competitors and provided all of the thrills and drama of a suspenseful movie. Dianne Durham had been fighting injuries during most of 1983 and had just recovered from knee surgery in time for the U.S.A. Championships in May 1984. Performing solidly before a hometown crowd in nearby Chicago, she finished in a fairly secure sixth place. One month later at the Olympic trials in Jacksonville, Florida, Dianne was still in sixth place after the first day's compulsory round. Disaster struck on the second day, however, when Durham was performing her optional vault. She landed crookedly on her left ankle and sprained it badly.

If an athlete is injured at the trials, the rules allow her to use 100 percent of her Championship score in the final rankings. But Dianne's score at the Championships was simply not high enough to keep her in the top eight. She finished ninth and did not make the Olympic team.

The woman who benefited most from Durham's misfortune was Kathy Johnson. Twenty-four-year-old Johnson, the oldest competitor trying out for the Olympic team, had a long history of gymnastic achievements. In 1977, she had won the American Cup and had become the national champion, and she won a bronze medal in the floor exercise a year later at the World Championships. Johnson had made the 1980 Olympic team, finishing second in the trials that year, and now she wanted nothing more than to make the 1984 Olympic team and win a medal.

But Kathy almost didn't make it. Although she held a strong seventh-place finish after the U.S.A. Championships, Johnson seriously faltered in the compulsory segment of the Olympic trials. There she suffered not one, but two breaks during her routine on the uneven bars, and her score of 7.6 reflected her poor performance. Kathy slipped in the rankings and believed that her Olympic dream was shattered. "I thought it would take more than a miracle," she said of her chances to make the team.

But the miracle happened. Kathy, known for her grace and fluid movements, especially in the floor exercise, used the optional exercises as a last-ditch opportunity to show what she did best. Her optional program was excellent, second only to Mary Lou's, and earned Johnson a 9.9 on the floor routine. Kathy's strong finish won her the eighth-place position on the team roster. Another experienced gymnast, Tracee Talavera, had made the 1980 Olympic team when she was only 13. Talavera was strong on the balance beam, and her final score in the trials won her the sixth place on the team.

The second place on the Olympic team was won by Julianne McNamara. Eighteen-year-old McNamara, a two-time winner of the American Cup, had recently joined Karolyi's training camp. In the trials, she was awarded the best compulsory scores for her consistently correct moves and body positions. Mc-Namara's speciality was the uneven bars, and she hoped to win an Olympic medal in that event. Michelle Dusserre and Pamela Bileck of Garden Grove, California, the third and fourth place finishers, were also assured places on the team.

The other finishers in the top eight—Lucy Wener, Tracee Talavera, Marie Roethlisberger, and Kathy Johnson—reported to training camp and sweated out the selection of the final two members of the six-woman team. Talavera and Johnson were ultimately chosen because of their previous experience in international competition, and Roethlisberger was selected as the alternate. All three added depth to the U.S.A. team.

There had been little doubt that Mary Lou Retton would make the 1984 Olympic team, and she had come through the trials untouched by the drama and the tension of the competition for the other five team positions. But Retton's lack of pressure was short lived. One month before the Games, Mary Lou's right knee locked during practice. She was immediately flown to Richmond, Virginia, for arthroscopic surgery that removed some troublesome cartilage from her joint. Retton did not have time to recover slowly. Determined to go to the Olympics, she was at the gym working out the day after surgery. Overcoming pain, she proved how tough she really was.

The 1984 U.S.A. women gymnasts knew that one of their toughest competitors would be Rumania's Ecaterina Szabo.

32

By July 28, 1984, the day of the opening ceremonies for the XXIII Olympiad, Retton was ready to face her next challenge. And she soon had her hands full. Her most serious competition came from the Rumanian team. Nadia Comaneci, their past champion, was in the audience, and her presence seemed to inspire the team.

The Rumanians were represented by several accomplished gymnasts. Their national champion, 17-year-old Ecaterina Szabo, had won the bronze medal in the all-around finals at the 1983 World Championships. Laura Cutina had come in second behind Retton at the 1984 McDonald's American Cup. And Lavinia Agache had won two individual silver medals (to tie with Szabo) and one bronze at the 1983 World Championships.

The women's competition began on July 30, 1984, before an enthusiastic audience. The compulsory exercises were first, and the top five scores of each team would be added together for the team score. In addition to making up 50 percent of the final team scores, the compulsories also counted toward each gymnast's all-around score.

After the first day of competition, Rumania was first in the team standings with 196.15 points. The United States was second with 195.70 points, and China was third with 194.15. Ecaterina Szabo had scored the only perfect 10 of the day to snag the lead in the all-around competition. With compulsory scores totaling 39.55 points, she shared the lead with teammate Lavina Agache.

The race for the gold was on! Only a fraction of a point separated Mary Lou's all-around score from the score of the two Rumanian leaders. In third place with 39.50 points, Retton was followed by teammates Julianne McNamara in fourth place with 39.45 points and Kathy Johnson in fifth place with 39.10.

Mary Lou was flying before the home crowd, and the fans rallied behind her. Many felt that her routines, especially on the vault and in the floor exercise, were underrated by the judges. Retton's vault had been almost twice as high and as long as any other, and she felt she had deserved a 10 on her floor exercise. "It's the best floor I've ever done," she said later. "I reacted to the crowd. I played to the crowd, and they reacted to me." When she was given only 9.95 points, the fans booed the judges, and Retton had to be consoled by her teammates.

Retton and the rest of the U.S.A. team were worried that the judging would mar the competition. One Rumanian judge in particular, Julia Roterescu, consistently scored the U.S. gymnasts lower than the other judges did. For example, she gave Mary Lou's beam routine only a 9.4, while all of the other judges saw a 9.9. Don Peters, the U.S.A. coach, filed four protests on the first day, but his objections did not override the judge's low scores. (Fortunately, the judging system at the Olympics was designed to minimize the influence of a low-scoring judge. Four judges score each performance, but the high and the low scores are discarded. Then the remaining two scores are averaged for the final score.)

After the scoring problems of the first day, Mary Lou knew she would not be given any advantages from the judges. She would have to earn every point by giving the best performance of her life. Determined to advance in the standings, Retton rose to the challenge in the optional exercises on August 1. In the optionals, each gymnast designs her own routines to best demonstrate her unique talents and strengths.

Retton used the optional exercises to her advantage and scored a perfect 10 in the vault—the first 10 ever awarded a U.S. woman in Olympic gymnastics! By the end of the second day of competition, she led the individual scores with 79.05 points. Ecaterina Szabo had also received a 10 on her optional vault but was now in second place with 78.75 points. Julianne McNamara collected 10s in the uneven bars and the floor exercise, but she fell from the beam and ended up in third place with 78.40 points. Kathy Johnson slipped to sixth place.

In the optional exercises, Julianne McNamara scored 10s in both the uneven bars *(above)* and the floor exercise *(right)*.

Members of the U.S.A. silver medal team *(left to right)*—Pamela Bileck, Tracee Talavera, Kathy Johnson, and Julianne McNamara —on the victory stand with the winning Rumanian gymnasts *(center)* and the third place team from China

The optional scores also counted for 50 percent of the final team scores, and the results gave Rumania the gold medal. The U.S.A. earned the silver and China the bronze. The women's second-place finish was the best performance ever by a United States' team in international competition. But after the men's victory of the previous day, the women's silver seemed a bit disappointing.

The U.S.A. men's gymnastics team *(left to right)*—Bart Conner, Peter Vidmar, James Hartung, Mitch Gaylord, Scott Johnson, and Tim Daggett—celebrate their first place team finish.

Both Bart Conner *(left)* and Peter Vidmar *(center)* were awarded gold medals in the individual competition.

40

It would have been difficult to follow in the footsteps of the men's gymnastics team, who had won the Olympic gold medal in a stunning upset victory over the highly favored world champions from China. This was the U.S. men's first team medal since the silver in the 1932 Olympic Games! After Peter Vidmar and Mitch Gaylord had scored perfect 10s in the opening compulsory rounds, the U.S.A. unexpectedly led in the team standings. Then during the optional exercises on July 31, the Americans were awarded three more perfect scores to clinch the gold medal.

The 1984 men's team showed considerable depth, and five of the six members were ranked among the top ten in the individual all-around standings after the first two days of competition. Peter Vidmar led with 118.55 points, Bart Conner was 4th with 118.30 points, Mitch Gaylord was 6th with 118.15 points, Tim Daggett was 8th with 117.85 points, and James Hartung was 9th with 117.75 points. Scott Johnson, the other member of the team, finished in 16th place with 116.60 points.

Two of the United States' men went on to win gold medals in the individual apparatus finals: Peter Vidmar scored a 10 on the men's pommel horse, and Bart Conner took a 10 on the parallel bars. The men's team also collected two individual silver and three bronze medals. The sellout crowds at Pauley Pavilion were expecting comparable achievements from Mary Lou and her teammates, and the pressure to measure up to these expectations was tremendous.

Going into the all-around finals on August 3, Retton was determined not to lose her precarious lead. Before the competition began, the combined scores from the compulsory and the optional rounds were halved, which cut Mary Lou's lead over Ecaterina Szabo to a mere .15 point. The points earned during the final round would be added to this score to determine the all-around winner.

The spotlight stayed on Retton and Szabo as they vied for the gold medal in the all-around competition, and the very first round set the stage for the heart-stopping performances that were to follow. Ecaterina opened the competition on the balance beam. Flawlessly, she executed four backflips in succession, a move so difficult that no other gymnast in the world even attempted it. Her performance commanded a perfect 10. Now it was Mary Lou's turn to respond.

Retton opened on the uneven bars. The highlight of her routine was the Retton *salto,* a difficult maneuver that she had invented. While executing the *salto,* Mary Lou swung down from a handstand on the high bar, slamming her midsection into the low bar and rebounding with such energy that she could release the bar and go into a front pike somersault. Then, almost miraculously, she would land seated on the high bar. While Retton's performance was dazzling, she took a step on her dismount, which lowered her score to 9.85. After only one round, Mary Lou had lost her thin .15 point lead over Szabo, and their scores were now tied at 49.375.

On the second rotation, Retton was on the balance beam, her least favorite apparatus. Few gymnasts like the four-inch wide beam because it is simply too easy to fall off. Mary Lou's routine included a spectacular stag leap mount and a daring backward tuck somersault. But because she wavered twice, she scored only 9.8 points. Meanwhile, Ecaterina performed a rousing floor routine that ended with music from "The Battle Hymn of the Republic." Her score of 9.95 put her ahead of Retton, 59.325 to 59.175.

Mary Lou was not concerned by Szabo's lead. "I knew she had me edged on points," she said. "But I also knew that I had the floor exercise and the vault coming up. And they are my two strong events."

Beginning her floor exercise with a high double back somersault in the layout position, Mary Lou awed the crowd by executing some of gymnastic's most difficult tumbling passes. For her daring performance, Retton earned a 10. Ecaterina managed a 9.9 on the vault, so now she was ahead by only .05 point.

After Ecaterina's strong showing on the beam, on the vault, and in the floor exercise *(above),* Mary Lou knew that she would have to complete a perfect vault *(right)* to win the all-around title.

The vault, Mary Lou's best event, was left. But Szabo's next event, the uneven bars, had won her the gold at the 1983 European Championships and second at the World Championships. Ecaterina executed an excellent routine but took a step on her landing and scored a 9.9. Retton knew that she needed a 9.95 to tie for the gold or a perfect 10 to win.

44

Mary Lou's vault was a unique version of the difficult Tsukahara vault, named after the Japanese men's champion who had invented it. The regular Tsukahara has the gymnast execute a half twist onto the horse and then complete a one-and-one-half back somersault before landing. Retton had built enough speed into her approach to allow her to travel in the air higher and farther than any other woman gymnast. The extra time spent in the air gave her seconds enough to add another full twist after the back somersault.

With all eyes in the auditorium turned on her, Mary Lou took a deep breath and accelerated down the runway. Even before she had landed, she knew she had executed a perfect vault, and she didn't even wait for the 10 to flash on the scoreboard before raising her arms in a powerful victory salute. She had done it! She had won the gold medal!

Then, as if to squash any doubts about deserving the gold, Retton walked back out to the runway to perform her second required vault. Another flawless performance! Another perfect 10!

With that last-minute, come-from-behind victory, Mary Lou had become the first U.S. woman ever to win an Olympic gold medal. She was the best gymnast in the world!

August 5 marked the final day of gymnastics competition at the 1984 Olympic Games. The gymnasts

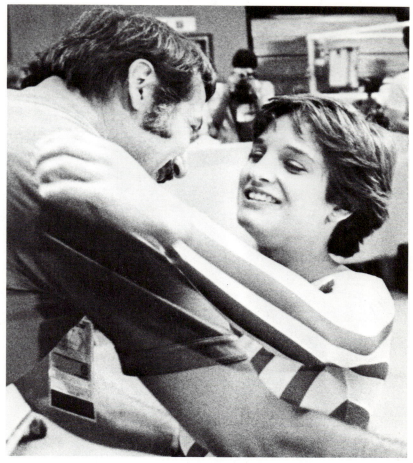

"The world's best gymnast" is congratulated by her happy coach.

with the eight best scores on each apparatus after the earlier compulsory and the optional rounds were scheduled to compete in the individual event finals.

Ecaterina Szabo tied with her teammate Simona Pauca *(right)* for gold medals in the balance beam competition.

The combined optional-compulsory scores were halved and then added to the scores earned on the last day. Medals were awarded on each apparatus.

The results of the individual event finals were anticlimactic after Retton's unprecedented gold medal in the all-around event. Affectionately called "The Golden Girl of Gymnastics," Retton did not win any more gold medals. Instead it was Ecaterina Szabo, the silver medalist in the all-around, who cashed in on the gold on the final day of competiton. She placed first in three events: the vault, the floor exercise, and the beam, in which she tied with teammate Simona Pauca.

The U.S.A. did win one gold medal when Julianne McNamara earned a 10 on the uneven bars to tie for first place with Ma Yanhong of China. McNamara also won a silver medal on the floor exercise, and Kathy Johnson realized an Olympic dream when she won a bronze on the balance beam.

Mary Lou Retton finished with three more individual medals—a silver on the vault and bronze medals on the uneven bars and in the floor exercise. She left the Games with five medals, the most won by any United States' athlete.

Mary Lou returned home a champion. When she arrived in West Virginia, she was greeted by Governor Jay Rockefeller. Her homecoming to Fairmont was marked by a three-hour parade, and friends and admirers lined the street for five miles to welcome her. A street in Fairmont was named after her.

Following the Olympics, Retton was kept busy with invitations for public appearances, interviews on television shows, and commercial endorsements for such companies as McDonald's, Vidal Sassoon, and General Mills. Mary Lou also met President Ronald Reagan and was one of the presenters at the 1984 Emmy Awards. She appeared on the cover of Sports Illustrated and was

After her visit to Fairmont, Mary Lou joined her fellow Olympians for a ceremony at the Capitol in Washington, D.C., where a crowd of more than 25,000 gathered to honor the U.S. athletes.

Among Retton's many interviews was an appearance on "The Tonight Show" with host Joan Rivers.

named 1984 Female Athlete of the Year by the Associated Press.

Mary Lou didn't stop breaking records once the Olympics were over. In March of 1985, just seven months after her Olympic triumph, Retton became the first female gymnast ever to win the McDonald's American Cup all-around title three times. She continued to train with Bela Karolyi in Houston, where she shared an apartment with her brother Ronnie.

51

SISKIYOU COUNTY SCHOOLS LIBRARY

The two top U.S. women gymnasts, Mary Lou Retton and Julianne McNamara, congratulate each other on another medal-winning performance.

52

Although Mary Lou plans to continue her gymnastics competition, no one knows what her future will bring. Like all athletes, she is always vulnerable to injuries that could shorten her career. And even if she remains healthy, a gymnast today has a relatively short career. Already, there are young, talented gymnasts who are setting their sights on overtaking her.

For Mary Lou Retton and many of the other 1984 Olympic champions, bringing a new interest to their sport was just as important as winning medals. Perhaps Bart Conner, gold medal gymnast and three-time Olympic team member, said it best. "I hope this changes things. For a sport to get a following, it has to have heroes. Look what Nadia did for gymnastics. Who ever knew where Rumania was before she came along? Now we have Americans who have had success."

Mary Lou Retton, whose bubbly, outgoing personality so captivated the hearts of Americans, is one of those success stories. It is unlikely that she will soon fade from the limelight, and her memorable performances will inspire young gymnasts for years to come.

Left to right: Tracee Talavera, Pamela Bileck, Julianne McNamara, and Kathy Johnson, members of the 1984 U.S.A. women's gymnastics team

THE WINNERS IN WOMEN'S GYMNASTICS - 1984 SUMMER OLYMPICS

ALL-AROUND
Gold MARY LOU RETTON, U.S.A.
Silver Ecaterina Szabo, Rumania
Bronze Simona Pauca, Rumania

TEAM
Rumania
U.S.A.
China

VAULT
Gold Ecaterina Szabo, Rumania
Silver MARY LOU RETTON, U.S.A.
Bronze Lavinia Agache, Rumania

FLOOR EXERCISES
Ecaterina Szabo, Rumania
JULIANNE McNAMARA, U.S.A.
MARY LOU RETTON, U.S.A.

UNEVEN PARALLEL BARS
Gold Ma Yanhonig, China
Gold JULIANNE McNAMARA, U.S.A.
Bronze MARY LOU RETTON, U.S.A.

BALANCE BEAM
Simona Pauca, Rumania
Ecaterina Szabo, Rumania
KATHY JOHNSON, U.S.A.

ACKNOWLEDGMENTS: The photographs are reproduced through the courtesy of: pp. 1, 38, UPI/Bettmann Archive; pp. 2, 6, 9, 10, 14, 15, 18, 19, 20, 23, 24, 26, 32, 36, 37, 39, 40, 44, 45, 47, 48, 50, 51, 52, 54, AP/Wide World Photos. Cover photo © 1984 by Robert Long/LPI.